My First
Biography

Abraham Lincoln

by Marion Dane Bauer
Illustrated by Liz Goulet Dubois

SCHOLASTIC INC.
New York   Toronto   London   Auckland
Sydney   Mexico City   New Delhi   Hong Kong

ISBN 978-0-545-34294-0

Text copyright © 2012 by Marion Dane Bauer
Illustrations copyright © 2012 by Liz Goulet Dubois

All rights reserved. Published by Scholastic Inc.
SCHOLASTIC and associated logos are trademarks and/or registered trademarks of Scholastic Inc.

12 11 10 9 8 7 6 5 4 3 2 1   12 13 14 15 16 17/0
Printed in the U.S.A.   40
First printing, January 2012

Book design by Jennifer Rinaldi Windau

Abraham Lincoln never expected to become president of the United States.

Kentucky, 1809

He was born in the wilderness in a log cabin.
His family was uneducated and poor,
but they all worked hard.

He was "a tall spider of a boy." When he was only eight years old, he helped his father clear the land with an ax.

Lincoln once said he got his education "by littles."

That meant he and his sister, Sarah, went to school only when they weren't needed to work at home.

He read and read to teach himself all he wanted to know.

He even taught himself to be a lawyer.

Lincoln once traveled from Illinois to Kentucky, where he saw slaves chained together. He knew slavery was wrong.

Many in the North wanted to change
the country's laws so that no one could own slaves.

Many in the South wanted to divide
the United States—half slave, half free.

Lincoln ran for president because he wanted the country to stay whole and for slaves to be free.

The Lincoln-Douglas debates, 1858

A lot of people were surprised when Lincoln won.
How could a man born in a log cabin be president?

The Southern states were unhappy. They decided to form their own country where they could own slaves. They attacked the North.

The First Battle of Bull Run, 1861

Lincoln declared war on
the states that had left the Union.
He said the country must remain whole.

The Battle of Antietam, 1862

The Civil War lasted four long, hard years.
Everyone suffered.

But Abraham Lincoln believed in the United States of America. In a famous speech at Gettysburg, he promised that this nation would remain free.

The Gettysburg Address, 1863

And it did! As soon as the North began to win, our 16th president signed a law that freed every slave.

Lincoln signs the Emancipation Proclamation, 1863

"If ever my name goes into history," he said,
"it will be for this act."